MY FIRST BO

BELGIUM

ALL ABOUT BELGIUM FOR KIDS

GL BED
CHILDREN BOOKS

Interior and cover Design: Daniel Day
Editor: Margaret Bam

For My Sons, Daniel, David and Jude

Grote Markt, Antwerp, Belgium

Belgium

Belgium is a **country**.

A country is land that is controlled by a **single government**. Countries are also called **nations, states, or nation-states**.

Countries can be **different sizes**. Some countries are big and others are small.

Grand Place, Brussels, Belgium

Where Is Belgium?

Belgium is located in the continent of Europe.

A continent is **a massive area of land that is separated from others by water or other natural features**.

Belgium is situated in the western part of Europe.

Brussels skyline and city hall tower, Belgium

Capital

The capital of Belgium is Brussels.

Brussels is located in the **northern-central part** of the country.

Antwerp is the largest city in Belgium.

Parc du Cinquantenaire, Belgium

Provinces

Belgium is a country that is made up of 10 provinces.

The provinces of Belgium are as follows:

Antwerp, Brabant, West Flanders, East Flanders, Hainaut, Liège, Limburg, Luxembourg, Namur and Walloon Brabant.

Ghent Canal, Belgium

Population

Belgium has population of around **11.5 million people** making it the 81st most populated country in the world and the 11th most populated country in Europe.

The Walzin Castle, Belgium

Size

Belgium is **30,528 square kilometres** making it the 34th largest country in Europe by area.

Belgium is the 140th largest country in the world.

Languages

The official languages of Belgium are Dutch, French and German. Dutch is the most widely spoken language in Belgium. French is spoken by the majority in the southern region of Wallonia and German is spoken by a small minority of the population living in the eastern part of Belgium.

Here are a few Dutch phrases
- **Goeiedag** - Hello
- **Goeden avond** - Good Morning

Grand Place, Brussels, Belgium

Attractions

There are lots of interesting places to see in Belgium.

Some beautiful places to visit in Belgium are

- Grand Place
- Belfry of Bruges
- Gravensteen
- Saint Bavo's Cathedral
- Atomium
- Parc du Cinquantenaire

Dinant, Belgium

History of Belgium

Belgium has a fascinating history. It was first inhabited by ancient tribes, and over time it was conquered and ruled by many different people. In the Middle Ages, it was part of the powerful Holy Roman Empire.

In the 19th century, Belgium grew rapidly, with many new cities and industries and becoming famous for its delicious chocolate, waffles, and beer.

Belgium gained independence on 4th October 1830.

Customs in Belgium

Belgium has many fascinating customs and traditions.

- Beer is a very popular drink and plays a prominent role in Belgian culture. There are around 1,500 types of beer in Belgium and 261 breweries where brewing skills and techniques are passed on from generation to generation.
- In the town of Oostduinkerke in West Flanders, many locals take part in horseback shrimp fishing.

St. Salvator's Cathedral, Bruges, Belgium

Music of Belgium

There are many different music genres in Belgium such as Rock music, Belgian hip hop, Blues, Experimental music, Industrial music, Electronic body music, Synth-pop and Psychedelic rock.

Some notable Belgian musicians include
- Lara Fabian
- Stromae
- Toots Thielemans
- Praga Khan

Moules-Frites

Food of Belgium

Belgium is known for having delicious, flavoursome and rich dishes.

The national dish of Belgium is **Moules-Frites** which is a delicious main dish of mussels and French fries.

Food of Belgium

Some popular dishes in Belgium include

- Carbonade flamande or stoofvlees
- Sole meunière
- Chicons au gratin
- Moules frites
- Stoemp

Atomium, Brussels

Weather in Belgium

Belgium has a temperate maritime climate with cool summers and mild winters.

The warmest months fall between June to September.

Groups of cows laying on Belgium Field

Animals of Belgium

There are many wonderful animals in Belgium.

Here are some animals that live in Belgium

- Foxes
- Badgers
- Weasels
- Beavers
- Seals
- Red deers

Ostend Beach, Belgium

Beaches

There are many beautiful beaches in Belgium which is one of the reasons why so many people visit this beautiful country every year.

Here are some of Belgium's beaches

- Ostend
- De Panne
- Blankenberg
- De Haan
- Oostduinkerke

Belgium football fan

Sports of Belgium

Sports play an integral part in Belgian culture. The most popular sport is Football.

Here are some of famous sportspeople from Belgium

- **Annie Lambrechts - Rollerskating**
- **Axel Witsel - Football**
- **Vincent Kompany - Football**
- **Youri Tielemans - Football**
- **Dedryck Boyata - Football**

Adolphe Sax (1814-1894)

Famous

Many successful people hail from Belgium.

Here are some notable Belgian figures

- **René Magritte – Artist**
- **Hergé – Cartoonist**
- **Adolphe Sax – Inventor**
- **Django Reinhardt – Guitarist**
- **Georges Lemaître – Priest**

The Rozenhoedkaai Canal, Bruges, Belgium

Something Extra...

As a little something extra, we are going to share some lesser known facts about Belgium.

- Famous actress, Audrey Hepburn, was born in Brussels.
- Belgium is one of the world's largest producers of chocolate, producing more than 220,000 tons per annum.

Words From the Author

We hope that you enjoyed learning about the wonderful country of Belgium.

Belgium is a country rich in culture and beauty, with lots of wonderful places to visit and people to meet.

We hope you continue to learn more about this wonderful nation. If you enjoyed this book, consider leaving a review!

With Love

Printed in Great Britain
by Amazon

21942150R00027